THE BRAIN GAME

TEST YOURSELF AND FRIENDS WITH BRAIN BUSTING PUZZLES!

Published and distributed by Imagination,
6161 Santa Monica Boulevard, Suite 100, Los Angeles
CA 90038, USA; Suite 1.14 Network House,
Bradfield Close, Woking GU22 7RE, UK and
64 North Terrace, Kent Town SA 5067, Australia.
www.imaginationgames.com

First Printing 2007
5 4 3 2 1

Printed in Canada

ISBN(10) – 1-934524-08-5
ISBN(13) – 978-1-934524-08-4

We would be happy to hear your questions or
comments about this book. Write to: Imagination,
Consumer Advice Department, 64 North Terrace,
Kent Town, South Australia, 5067, Australia
or email contactus@imaginationgames.com

Contents

Introduction

Welcome to the game that proves that these days, most brains are the victims of chronic unemployment.

With 20 completely different games full of questions, puzzles and mind-bending challenges, we'll get your brain back into full-time work and find out where you rate on the Brain Scale.

Are you a Don or a Dunce ... an Einstein or a Frankenstein? In actual fact, it doesn't really matter, because The Brain Game is designed to train your brain to work harder than ever before. The more you play, the smarter you'll get.

In the end, when your brain's as blunt as your pencil and the scores are on the board, where will your name be ... in the Hall of Fame or the dreaded Hall of Shame?

The only way to find out is to put your neck-top computer into hyper-drive and accept the ultimate challenge from the quiz book that thinks it's an IQ test.

How to play

It's all quite simple really (actually it's not, but that's the whole point). All 20 games consist of 6 mind-bending puzzles worth a total of 100 points. As a game goes on the puzzles get harder but they're worth more points! If you don't want to mark your book, have spare paper handy to mark down your answers.

Single Player Game
If you're playing solo, pick a game and complete all the puzzles from 1-6, recording your answers on paper or in the book. When you come to Puzzle 6, the Sudoku Challenge, you must complete the entire puzzle by filling in all the missing numbers.

Multi Player Game
If you're brave enough to play with friends, everyone needs some paper to record their answers. This time in the Sudoku Challenge, players need only try to identify the one number missing from the square indicated, rather than complete the whole puzzle.

Scoring
The answers are on the last page of each game, and depending on the puzzle difficulty, you can score 5, 10, 15, 25 or 35 points for correct answers. Add up your score and check it against the Brain Scale to see whether your brains should be crumbed or congratulated.

Depending on your ego, honesty and humility, high scores can be recorded in the Hall of Fame, hopeless scores in the Hall of Shame. And if all that really is too easy, try adding a time limit to every question.

Game One

Here's the first game of six puzzles. Write your answers down, then after the final puzzle, check your results on the answers page. Total your points to see where you rate on the Brain Scale. Good luck!

Puzzle One

Cognitive Therapy - 5 points for a correct answer

Puzzle Two

Match Shape - 10 points for a correct answer

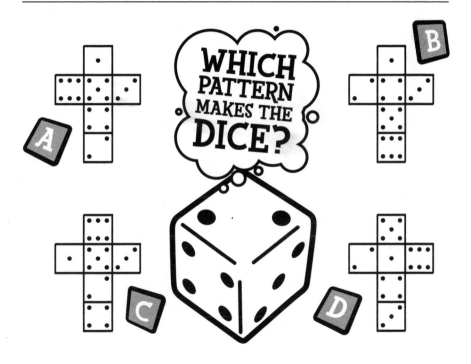

Puzzle Three

Word Puzzle - 10 points for a correct answer

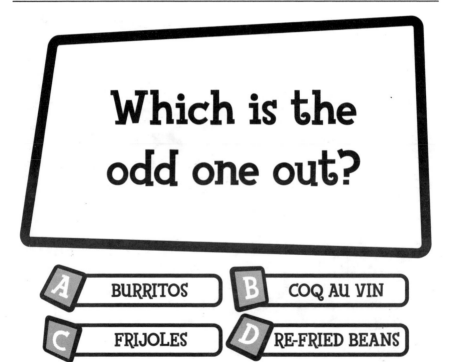

Which is the odd one out?

A BURRITOS

B COQ AU VIN

C FRIJOLES

D RE-FRIED BEANS

Puzzle Four

Maths Riddle - 15 points for a correct answer

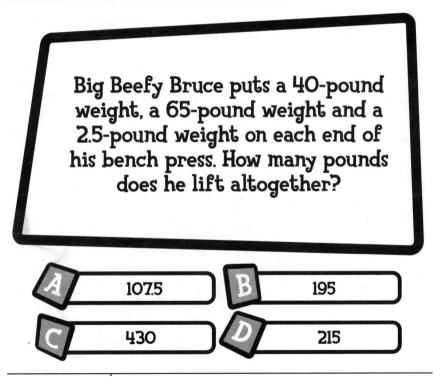

Big Beefy Bruce puts a 40-pound weight, a 65-pound weight and a 2.5-pound weight on each end of his bench press. How many pounds does he lift altogether?

A 107.5

B 195

C 430

D 215

Puzzle Five

Number Puzzle - 25 points for a correct answer

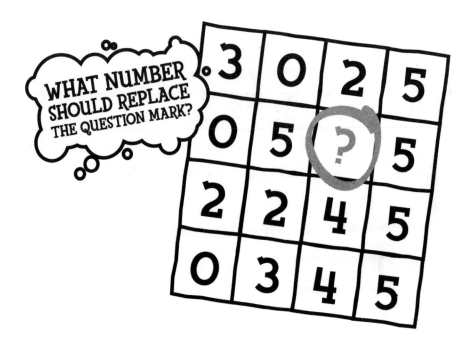

Puzzle Six

Sudoku Puzzle - 35 points for a correct answer

USE YOUR POWERS OF DEDUCTION TO SOLVE THE COMPLETE SUDOKU GRID

IF MORE THAN ONE PERSON IS PLAYING SIMPLY FIND THE MISSING NUMBER

Game One - Answers

Here's where we define the intellectuals from the in-to-nothing-at-alls.

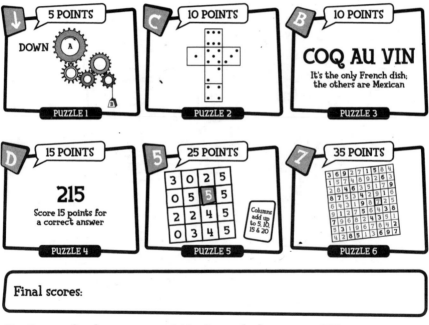

PUZZLE 1 — 5 POINTS
DOWN

PUZZLE 2 — 10 POINTS

PUZZLE 3 — 10 POINTS
COQ AU VIN
It's the only French dish;
the others are Mexican

PUZZLE 4 — 15 POINTS
215
Score 15 points for
a correct answer

PUZZLE 5 — 25 POINTS
Columns
add up
to 5, 10,
15 & 20

PUZZLE 6 — 35 POINTS

Final scores:

Check your final score against the Brain Scale on page 167.

Game Two

No matter how smart you are, it doesn't pay to let your brains go to your head. Once again, write your answers down, then after the final puzzle, check your results on the answers page. Total your points to see if you've moved up or down on the Brain Scale.

Puzzle One

Brain Maze - 5 points for a correct answer

Puzzle Two

Weights/Values - 10 points for a correct answer

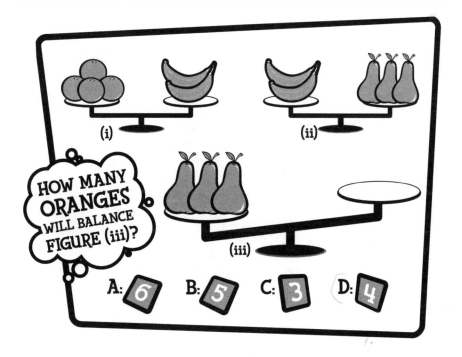

(i)

(ii)

HOW MANY ORANGES WILL BALANCE FIGURE (iii)?

(iii)

A: 6   B: 5   C: 3   D: 4

Puzzle Three

Word Grid - 10 points for a correct answer

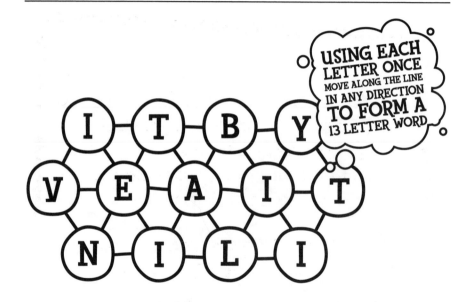

USING EACH LETTER ONCE MOVE ALONG THE LINE IN ANY DIRECTION TO FORM A 13 LETTER WORD

Puzzle Four

Maths Riddle - 15 points for a correct answer

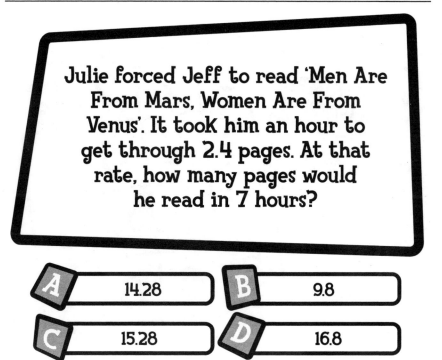

Julie forced Jeff to read 'Men Are From Mars, Women Are From Venus'. It took him an hour to get through 2.4 pages. At that rate, how many pages would he read in 7 hours?

A	14.28	B	9.8
C	15.28	D	16.8

Puzzle Five

Number Puzzle - 25 points for a correct answer

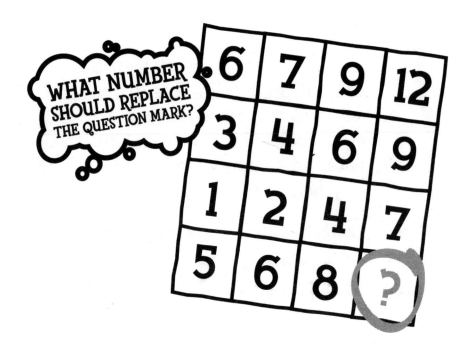

WHAT NUMBER SHOULD REPLACE THE QUESTION MARK?

6	7	9	12
3	4	6	9
1	2	4	7
5	6	8	?

Puzzle Six

Sudoku Puzzle - 35 points for a correct answer

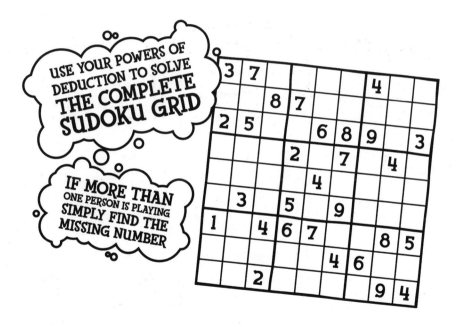

USE YOUR POWERS OF DEDUCTION TO SOLVE THE COMPLETE SUDOKU GRID

IF MORE THAN ONE PERSON IS PLAYING SIMPLY FIND THE MISSING NUMBER

Game Two - Answers

It's time to sort the scholars from the simpletons.

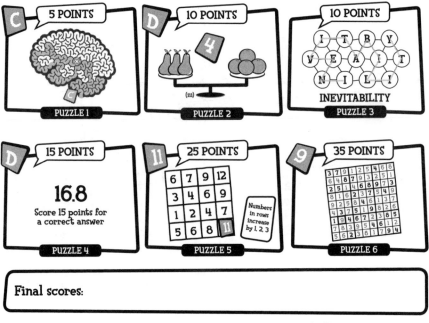

PUZZLE 1 — C — 5 POINTS

PUZZLE 2 — D — 10 POINTS — 4

PUZZLE 3 — 10 POINTS — INEVITABILITY

PUZZLE 4 — D — 15 POINTS — 16.8
Score 15 points for a correct answer

PUZZLE 5 — 11 — 25 POINTS

6	7	9	12
3	4	6	9
1	2	4	7
5	6	8	11

Numbers in rows increase by 1, 2, 3

PUZZLE 6 — 9 — 35 POINTS

Final scores:

Turn to page 167 to see where you rate on the Brain Scale.

Game Three

Has your brain been fried? We hope not, because you're about to need all the brain power you can muster.

Puzzle One

Brain Maze - 5 points for a correct answer

Puzzle Two

Match Shape - 10 points for a correct answer

Puzzle Three

Word Puzzle - 10 points for a correct answer

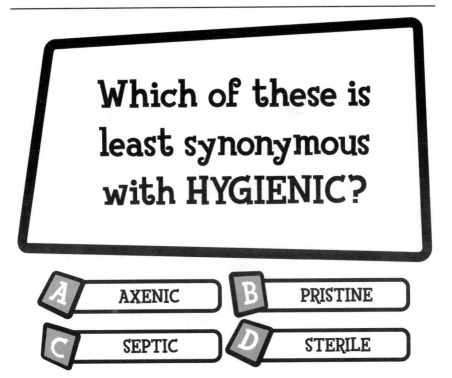

Which of these is least synonymous with HYGIENIC?

A. AXENIC

B. PRISTINE

C. SEPTIC

D. STERILE

Puzzle Four

Maths Riddle - 15 points for a correct answer

Michelle ate the same thing every day: fruit and yogurt for breakfast (85 calories), crab salad for lunch (305 calories) and lentil soup for dinner (170 calories).

How many calories did she consume in a week?

A 560

B 1845

C 2700

D 3920

Puzzle Five

Number Puzzle - 25 points for a correct answer

Puzzle Six

Sudoku Puzzle - 35 points for a correct answer

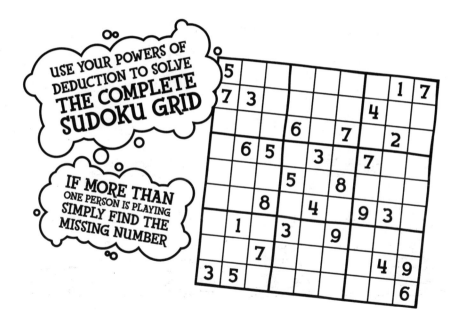

Game Three - Answers

Should your brain be crumbed or congratulated?

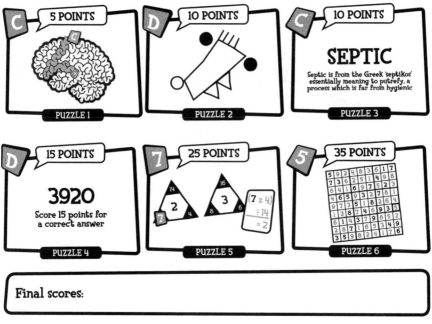

PUZZLE 1 — C — 5 POINTS

PUZZLE 2 — D — 10 POINTS

PUZZLE 3 — C — 10 POINTS
SEPTIC
Septic is from the Greek 'septikos' essentially meaning to putrefy, a process which is far from hygienic

PUZZLE 4 — D — 15 POINTS
3920
Score 15 points for a correct answer

PUZZLE 5 — 7 — 25 POINTS
14, 2, 4 | 16, 3, 8, 6 | (7 x 4) ÷ 14 = 2

PUZZLE 6 — 5 — 35 POINTS

Final scores:

Go to page 167 and check out where you rate on the Brain Scale.

Game Four

Oscar Wilde once said "I have nothing to declare except my genius". Then again, he'd never played The Brain Game.

Puzzle One

Cognitive Therapy - 5 points for a correct answer

Puzzle Two

Word Puzzle - 10 points for a correct answer

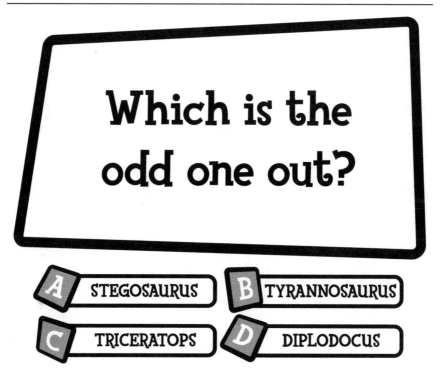

Which is the odd one out?

A STEGOSAURUS

B TYRANNOSAURUS

C TRICERATOPS

D DIPLODOCUS

Puzzle Three

Word Grid - 10 points for a correct answer

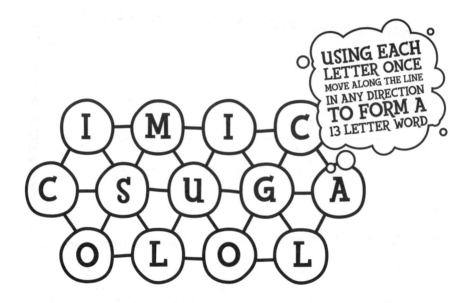

USING EACH LETTER ONCE MOVE ALONG THE LINE IN ANY DIRECTION TO FORM A 13 LETTER WORD

Puzzle Four

Maths Riddle - 15 points for a correct answer

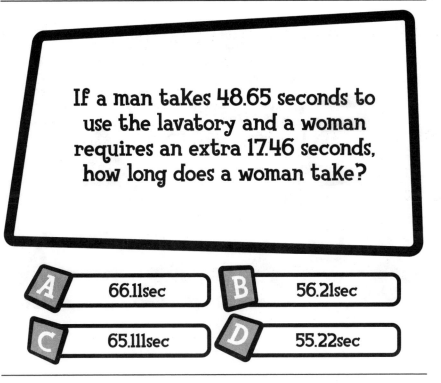

If a man takes 48.65 seconds to use the lavatory and a woman requires an extra 17.46 seconds, how long does a woman take?

A 66.11sec

B 56.21sec

C 65.111sec

D 55.22sec

Puzzle Five

Number Puzzle - 25 points for a correct answer

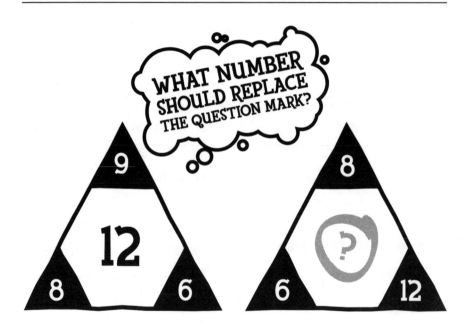

Puzzle Six

Sudoku Puzzle - 35 points for a correct answer

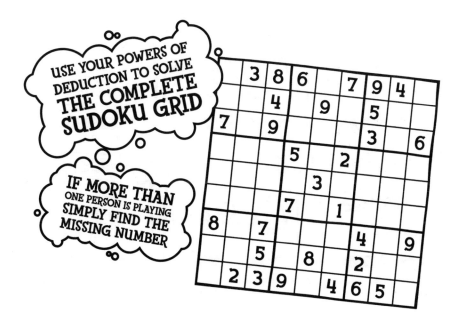

USE YOUR POWERS OF DEDUCTION TO SOLVE THE COMPLETE SUDOKU GRID

IF MORE THAN ONE PERSON IS PLAYING SIMPLY FIND THE MISSING NUMBER

Game Four - Answers

Here's where we define the intellectuals from the in-to-nothing-at-alls.

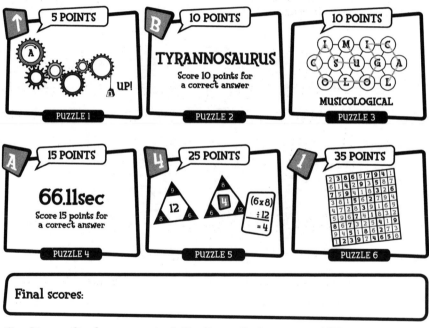

PUZZLE 1 — 5 POINTS — UP!

PUZZLE 2 — 10 POINTS — TYRANNOSAURUS
Score 10 points for a correct answer

PUZZLE 3 — 10 POINTS — MUSICOLOGICAL

PUZZLE 4 — 15 POINTS — 66.11sec
Score 15 points for a correct answer

PUZZLE 5 — 25 POINTS — 12, (6 x 8) ÷ 12 = 4

PUZZLE 6 — 35 POINTS

Final scores:

Check your final score against the Brain Scale on page 167.

Game Five

Brains are 85% water, which is why you may have steam coming out of your ears by now.

Puzzle One

Brain Maze - 5 points for a correct answer

Puzzle Two

Weight/Values - 10 points for a correct answer

(i)

(ii)

HOW MANY **APPLES** WILL BALANCE FIGURE (iii)?

(iii)

A: 3   B: 4   C: 2   D: 5

Puzzle Three

Word Puzzle - 10 points for a correct answer

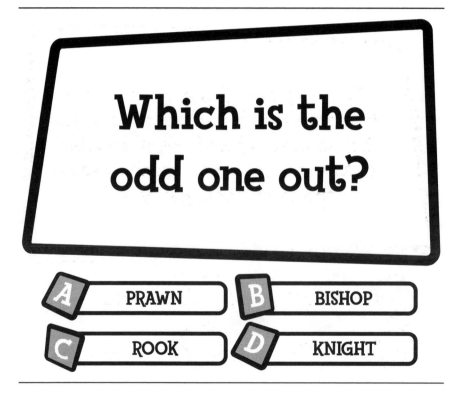

Which is the odd one out?

A PRAWN

B BISHOP

C ROOK

D KNIGHT

Puzzle Four

Maths Riddle - 15 points for a correct answer

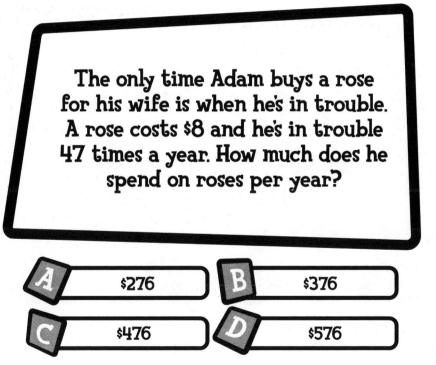

The only time Adam buys a rose for his wife is when he's in trouble. A rose costs $8 and he's in trouble 47 times a year. How much does he spend on roses per year?

A. $276

B. $376

C. $476

D. $576

Puzzle Five

Number Puzzle - 25 points for a correct answer

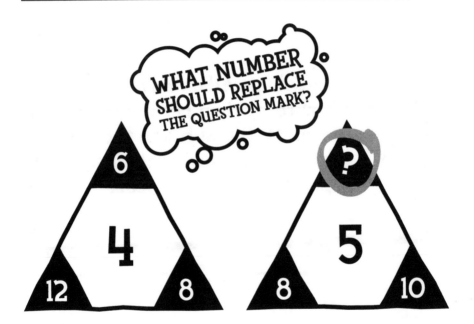

Puzzle Six

Sudoku Puzzle - 35 points for a correct answer

Game Five - Answers

It's time to see who wins the title of 'The Brainiest Brain in the Room'.

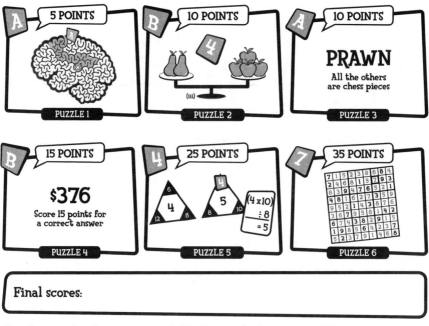

A | 5 POINTS | PUZZLE 1

B | 10 POINTS | PUZZLE 2

(iii)

A | 10 POINTS | PUZZLE 3

PRAWN

All the others
are chess pieces

B | 15 POINTS | PUZZLE 4

$376

Score 15 points for
a correct answer

25 POINTS | PUZZLE 5

$(4 \times 10) \div 8 = 5$

35 POINTS | PUZZLE 6

Final scores:

Check your final score against the Brain Scale on page 167

46

Game Six

Come on now, use your brain.
It's the little things that count.
You want to move up the Brain Scale, not slide down.

Puzzle One

Cognitive Therapy - 5 points for a correct answer

Puzzle Two

Match Shape - 10 points for a correct answer

Puzzle Three

Word Puzzle - 10 points for a correct answer

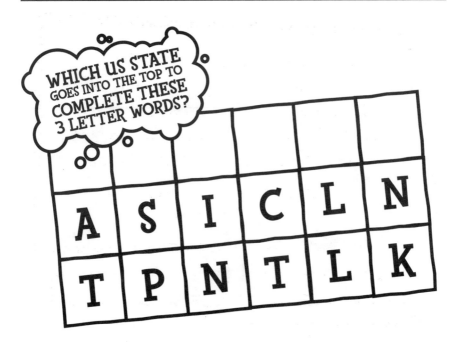

WHICH US STATE GOES INTO THE TOP TO COMPLETE THESE 3 LETTER WORDS?

A	S	I	C	L	N
T	P	N	T	L	K

Puzzle Four

Matha Riddle - 15 points for a correct answer

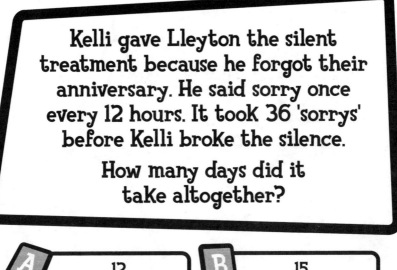

Kelli gave Lleyton the silent treatment because he forgot their anniversary. He said sorry once every 12 hours. It took 36 'sorrys' before Kelli broke the silence.

How many days did it take altogether?

A. 12

B. 15

C. 18

D. 21

Puzzle Five

Number Puzzle - 25 points for a correct answer

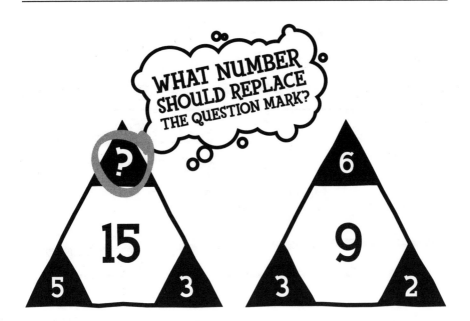

Puzzle Six

Sudoku Puzzle - 35 points for a correct answer

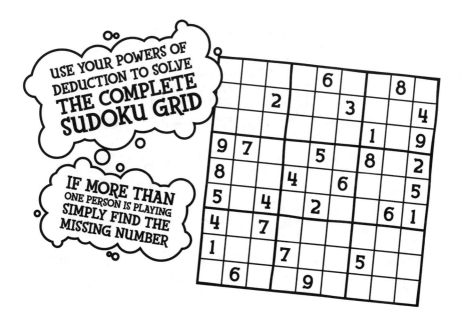

Game Six - Answers

OK ... are you an Einstein or a Frankenstein? ... an egghead or an air-head?

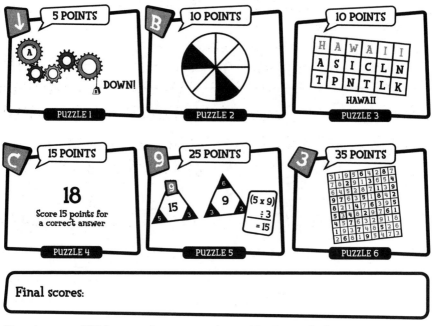

5 POINTS — PUZZLE 1 — DOWN!

10 POINTS — PUZZLE 2

10 POINTS — PUZZLE 3 — HAWAII

15 POINTS — PUZZLE 4
18
Score 15 points for a correct answer

25 POINTS — PUZZLE 5
(5×9)
$\div 3$
$= 15$

35 POINTS — PUZZLE 6

Final scores:

Turn to page 167 to see where you rate on the Brain Scale.

Game Seven

Some people think the human brain
is what we think we think with.
Here's your chance to prove you're one of them.

Puzzle One

Brain Maze - 5 points for a correct answer

Puzzle Two

Weights/Values - 10 points for a correct answer

Puzzle Three

Word Puzzle - 10 points for a correct answer

Puzzle Four

Maths Riddle - 15 points for a correct answer

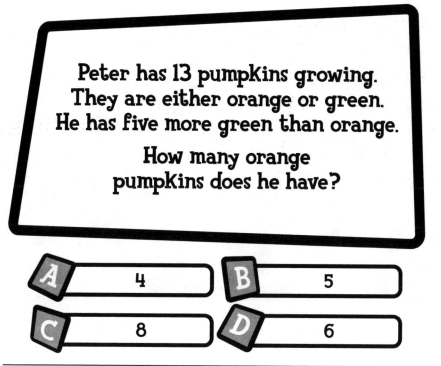

Peter has 13 pumpkins growing.
They are either orange or green.
He has five more green than orange.

How many orange
pumpkins does he have?

A 4

B 5

C 8

D 6

Puzzle Five

Number Puzzle - 25 points for a correct answer

Puzzle Six

Sudoku Puzzle - 35 points for a correct answer

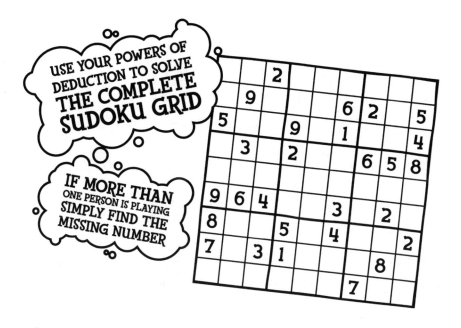

USE YOUR POWERS OF DEDUCTION TO SOLVE THE COMPLETE SUDOKU GRID

IF MORE THAN ONE PERSON IS PLAYING SIMPLY FIND THE MISSING NUMBER

Game Seven - Answers

Let's sort the dons from the dunces, the masterminds from the never-minds.

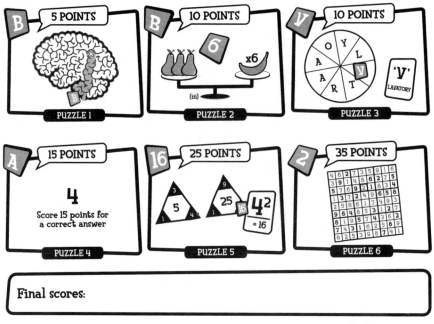

PUZZLE 1 — B — 5 POINTS

PUZZLE 2 — B — 10 POINTS

PUZZLE 3 — V — 10 POINTS — 'V' LAVATORY

PUZZLE 4 — A — 15 POINTS
4
Score 15 points for a correct answer

PUZZLE 5 — 16 — 25 POINTS
$4^2 = 16$

PUZZLE 6 — 2 — 35 POINTS

Final scores:

Go to page 167 and check out where you rate on the Brain Scale.

Game Eight

That neck-top computer of yours should be
up to speed by now. Go for it Giga-brain!

Puzzle One

Cognitive Therapy - 5 points for a correct answer

Puzzle Two

Match Shape - 10 points for a correct answer

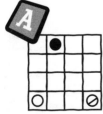
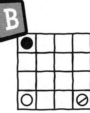
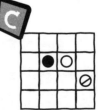

Puzzle Three

Word Puzzle - 10 points for a correct answer

Which of these is least synonymous with GENTLEMANLY?

A HOYDENISH

B CHIVALROUS

C GENTEEL

D COUTH

Puzzle Four

Maths Riddle - 15 points for a correct answer

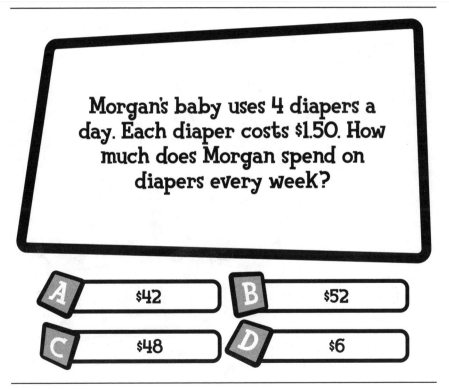

Morgan's baby uses 4 diapers a day. Each diaper costs $1.50. How much does Morgan spend on diapers every week?

A. $42

B. $52

C. $48

D. $6

Puzzle Five

Number Puzzle - 25 points for a correct answer

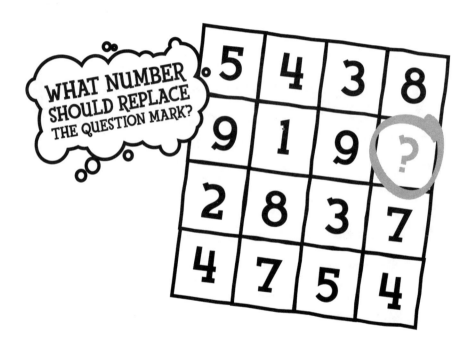

Puzzle Six

Sudoku Puzzle - 35 points for a correct answer

USE YOUR POWERS OF DEDUCTION TO SOLVE THE COMPLETE SUDOKU GRID

IF MORE THAN ONE PERSON IS PLAYING SIMPLY FIND THE MISSING NUMBER

Game Eight - Answers

Whose brain will reign supreme?
Remember! The more you play the smarter you'll become.

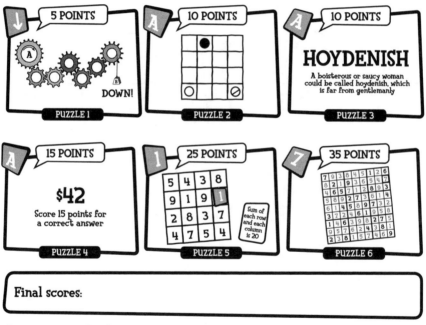

PUZZLE 1 — ↓ 5 POINTS — DOWN!

PUZZLE 2 — A 10 POINTS

PUZZLE 3 — A 10 POINTS — HOYDENISH — A boisterous or saucy woman could be called hoydenish, which is far from gentlemanly

PUZZLE 4 — A 15 POINTS — $42 — Score 15 points for a correct answer

PUZZLE 5 — 1 25 POINTS

5	4	3	8
9	1	9	1
2	8	3	7
4	7	5	4

Sum of each row and each column is 20

PUZZLE 6 — 7 35 POINTS

7	9	3	8	4	5	1	2	6
8	2	1	9	3	6	5	4	7
4	6	5	7	1	2	8	9	3
5	8	9	2	7	3	6	1	4
6	1	4	5	8	9	7	3	2
3	7	2	4	6	1	9	5	8
1	4	6	3	9	8	2	7	5
9	5	7	6	2	4	3	8	1
2	3	8	1	5	7	4	6	9

Final scores:

Compare your final score against the Brain Scale on page 167.

Game Nine

Remember, there's either Fame or Shame
at the end of every game.

Puzzle One

Brain Maze - 5 points for a correct answer

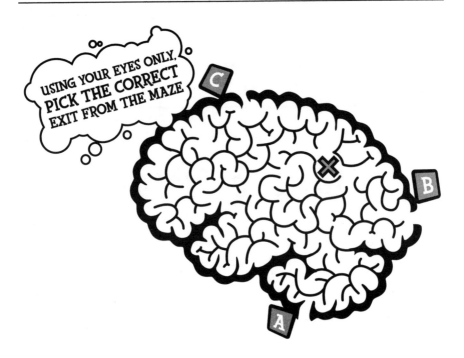

Puzzle Two

Weights/Values - 10 points for a correct answer

HOW MANY ORANGES WILL BALANCE FIGURE (iii)?

(i)
(ii)
(iii)

A: 4   B: 6   C: 2   D: 3

Puzzle Three

Word Puzzle - 10 points for a correct answer

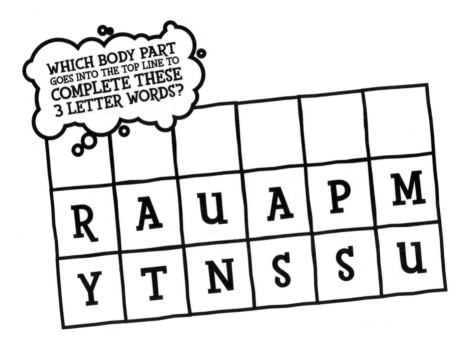

Puzzle Four

Maths Riddle - 15 points for a correct answer

Amanda and Nick are driving and discover they're lost. Nick refuses to ask for directions and spends the next 2.5 hours driving in the wrong direction at 24 mph. As a result, they are now how many miles further from their destination?

A 30

B 60

C 90

D 120

Puzzle Five

Number Puzzle - 25 points for a correct answer

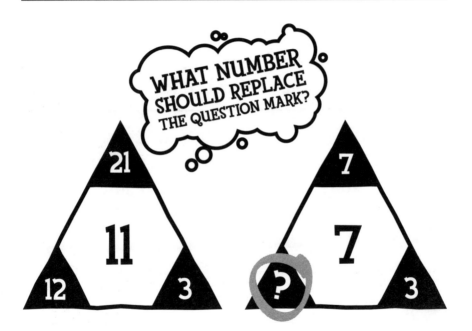

Puzzle Six

Sudoku Puzzle - 35 points for a correct answer

USE YOUR POWERS OF DEDUCTION TO SOLVE **THE COMPLETE SUDOKU GRID**

IF MORE THAN ONE PERSON IS PLAYING SIMPLY FIND THE MISSING NUMBER

Game Nine - Answers

Let's see what your brain is made of and where you sit on the evolutionary scale.

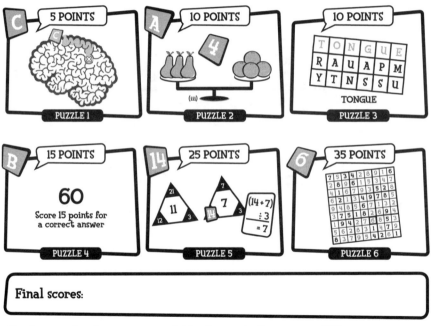

PUZZLE 1 — C — 5 POINTS

PUZZLE 2 — A — 10 POINTS — 4 — (iii)

PUZZLE 3 — 10 POINTS

T	O	N	G	U	E
R	A	U	A	P	M
Y	T	N	S	S	U

TONGUE

PUZZLE 4 — B — 15 POINTS

60

Score 15 points for a correct answer

PUZZLE 5 — 14 — 25 POINTS

21, 11, 12, 3 — 7, 7, 3 — 4 — (14 + 7) ÷ 3 = 7

PUZZLE 6 — 6 — 35 POINTS

Final scores:

Check your final score against the Brain Scale on page 167.

78

Game Ten

Unless some of your 100 billion neurons have lost their spark, you should be getting the idea by now.

Puzzle One

Cognitive Therapy - 5 points for a correct answer

Puzzle Two

Match Shape - 10 points for a correct answer

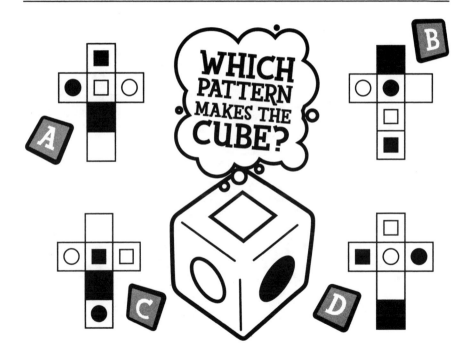

Puzzle Three

Word Grid - 10 points for a correct answer

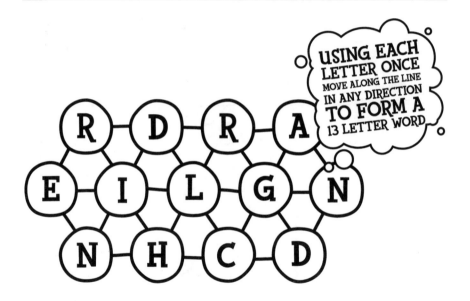

USING EACH LETTER ONCE MOVE ALONG THE LINE IN ANY DIRECTION TO FORM A 13 LETTER WORD

Puzzle Four

Maths Riddle - 15 points for a correct answer

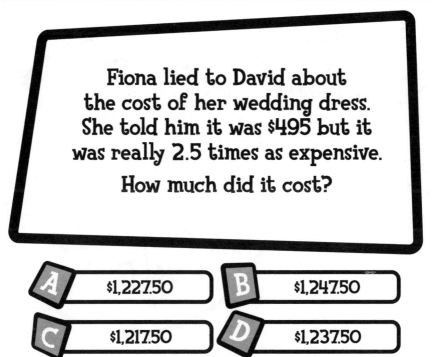

Fiona lied to David about
the cost of her wedding dress.
She told him it was $495 but it
was really 2.5 times as expensive.

How much did it cost?

A $1,227.50

B $1,247.50

C $1,217.50

D $1,237.50

Puzzle Five

Number Puzzle - 25 points for a correct answer

WHAT NUMBER SHOULD REPLACE THE QUESTION MARK?

Puzzle Six

SudokuPuzzle - 35 points for-a correct answer

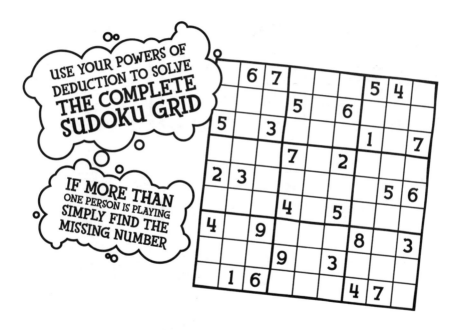

USE YOUR POWERS OF DEDUCTION TO SOLVE THE COMPLETE SUDOKU GRID

IF MORE THAN ONE PERSON IS PLAYING SIMPLY FIND THE MISSING NUMBER

Game Ten - Answers

Who's the smartest in the room? We'll find out as soon as you total your scores!

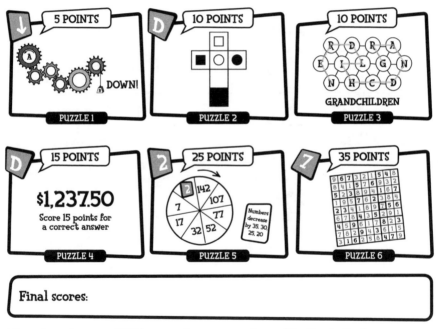

PUZZLE 1 — 5 POINTS — DOWN!

PUZZLE 2 — 10 POINTS

PUZZLE 3 — 10 POINTS — GRANDCHILDREN

PUZZLE 4 — 15 POINTS — $1,237.50 — Score 15 points for a correct answer

PUZZLE 5 — 25 POINTS — 142, 107, 77, 52, 32, 17, 7 — Numbers decrease by 35, 30, 25, 20

PUZZLE 6 — 35 POINTS

Final scores:

Then turn to page 167 to see where you rate on the Brain Scale.

Game Eleven

If your previous scores are the best you can do, you
obviously need more practice. How about 10 more games?

Puzzle One

Brain Maze - 5 points for a correct answer

Puzzle Two

Weights/Values - 10 points for a correct answer

(i)

(ii)

HOW MANY **PEARS** WILL BALANCE FIGURE (iii)?

(iii)

A: 3   B: 2   C: 4   D: 5

Puzzle Three

Word Puzzle - 10 points for a correct answer

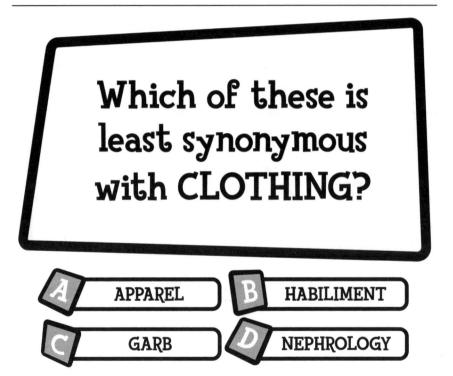

Which of these is least synonymous with CLOTHING?

A APPAREL

B HABILIMENT

C GARB

D NEPHROLOGY

Puzzle Four

Maths Riddle - 15 points for a correct answer

Stuart's fuel tank leaked at a rate of 10 gallons an hour. At 9am the tank contained 90 gallons. How many gallons did it contain at midday?

A 50

B 60

C 70

D 80

Puzzle Five

Number Puzzle - 25 points for a correct answer

Puzzle Six

Sudoku Puzzle - 35 points for a correct answer

USE YOUR POWERS OF DEDUCTION TO SOLVE THE COMPLETE SUDOKU GRID

IF MORE THAN ONE PERSON IS PLAYING SIMPLY FIND THE MISSING NUMBER

Game Eleven - Answers

OK ... are you an Einstein or a Frankenstein? ... an egghead or an air-head?

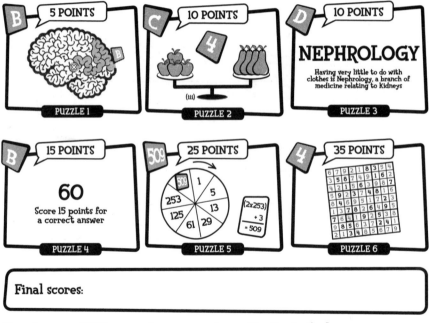

B 5 POINTS

PUZZLE 1

C 10 POINTS

4

(iii)

PUZZLE 2

D 10 POINTS

NEPHROLOGY

Having very little to do with clothes is Nephrology, a branch of medicine relating to kidneys

PUZZLE 3

B 15 POINTS

60

Score 15 points for a correct answer

PUZZLE 4

509 25 POINTS

509 1
5
253
13
125
61 29

(2x253) + 3 = 509

PUZZLE 5

4 35 POINTS

PUZZLE 6

Final scores:

Turn to page 167 to see where you rate on the Brain Scale.

Game Twelve

A lot of people are smarter than they look
- just as well, really. Best of luck with this game.

Puzzle One

Cognitive Therapy - 5 points for a correct answer

Puzzle Two

Match Shape - 10 points for a correct answer

Puzzle Three

Word Puzzle - 10 points for a correct answer

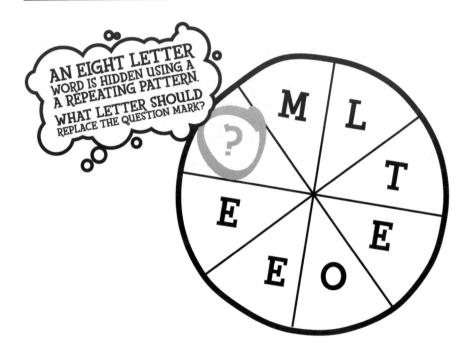

Puzzle Four

Maths Riddle - 15 points for a correct answer

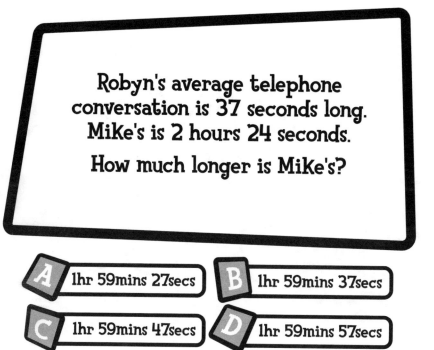

Robyn's average telephone conversation is 37 seconds long. Mike's is 2 hours 24 seconds.

How much longer is Mike's?

A 1hr 59mins 27secs

B 1hr 59mins 37secs

C 1hr 59mins 47secs

D 1hr 59mins 57secs

Puzzle Five

Number Puzzle - 25 points for a correct answer

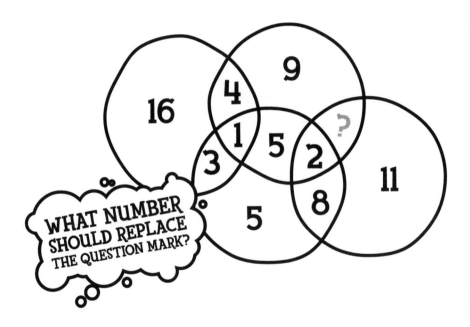

WHAT NUMBER SHOULD REPLACE THE QUESTION MARK?

Puzzle Six

Sudoku Puzzle - 35 points for a correct answer

Game Twelve - Answers

Here's where we define the intellectuals from the in-to-nothing-at-alls.

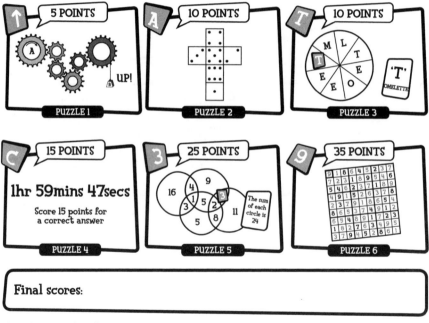

5 POINTS

UP!

PUZZLE 1

10 POINTS

PUZZLE 2

10 POINTS

'T'
OMELETTE

PUZZLE 3

15 POINTS

1hr 59mins 47secs

Score 15 points for a correct answer

PUZZLE 4

25 POINTS

16   9   4   1   5   2   3   3   5   8   11

The sum of each circle is 24

PUZZLE 5

35 POINTS

PUZZLE 6

Final scores:

Check your final score against the Brain Scale on page 167.

Game Thirteen

Some people have more luck than brains ... and this could be the game to prove it.

Puzzle One

Brain Maze - 5 points for a correct answer

Puzzle Two

Weights/Values - 10 points for a correct answer

(i) x8

(ii)

HOW MANY BANANAS WILL BALANCE FIGURE (iii)?

(iii)

A: 3   B: 5   C: 6   D: 4

Puzzle Three

Word Grid - 10 points for a correct answer

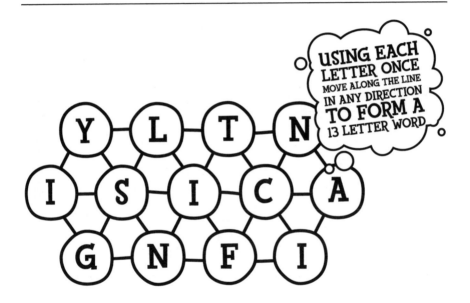

Puzzle Four

Maths Riddle - 15 points for a correct answer

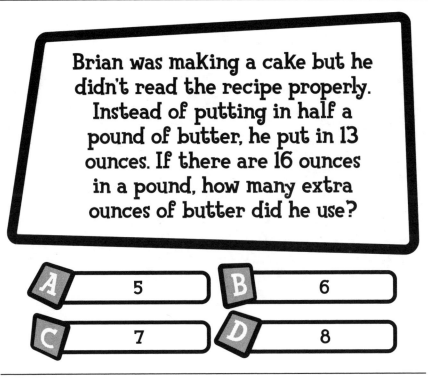

Brian was making a cake but he didn't read the recipe properly. Instead of putting in half a pound of butter, he put in 13 ounces. If there are 16 ounces in a pound, how many extra ounces of butter did he use?

A 5

B 6

C 7

D 8

Puzzle Five

Number Puzzle - 25 points for a correct answer

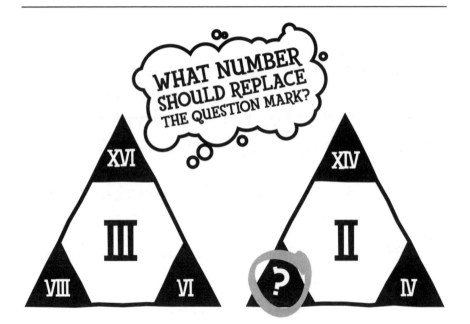

Puzzle Six

Sudoku Puzzle - 35 points for a correct answer

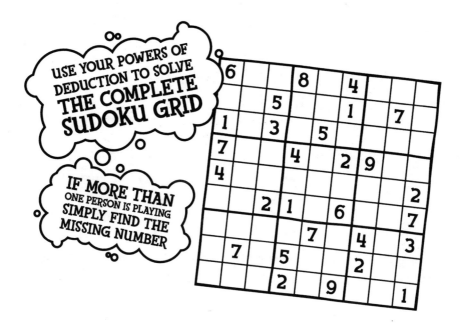

Game Thirteen - Answers

It's time to sort the scholars from the simpletons.

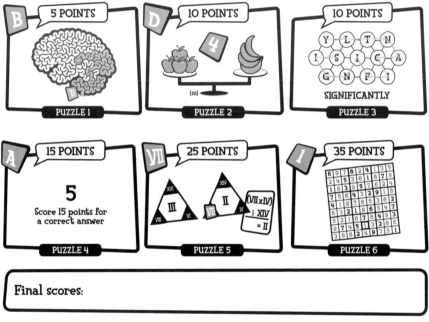

B 5 POINTS — PUZZLE 1

D 10 POINTS — PUZZLE 2

10 POINTS — PUZZLE 3
SIGNIFICANTLY

A 15 POINTS — PUZZLE 4
5
Score 15 points for a correct answer

VII 25 POINTS — PUZZLE 5
$(VII \times IV) \div XIV = II$

I 35 POINTS — PUZZLE 6

Final scores:

Turn to page 167 to see where you rate on the Brain Scale.

Game Fourteen

It's not enough just to be smart - you need to know when to be smart. So how about starting now?

Puzzle One

Cognitive Therapy - 5 points for a correct answer

Puzzle Two

Match Shape - 10 points for a correct answer

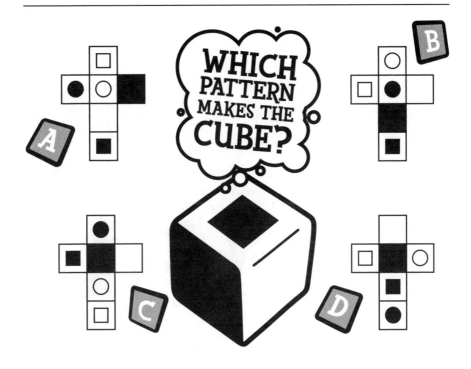

Puzzle Three

Word Puzzle - 10 points for a correct answer

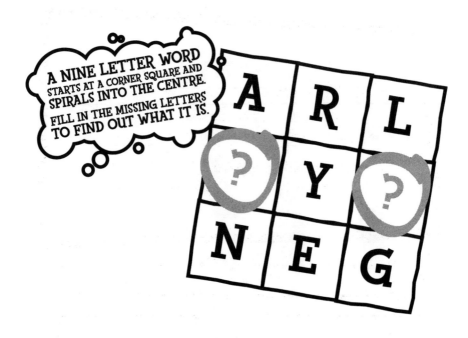

A NINE LETTER WORD STARTS AT A CORNER SQUARE AND SPIRALS INTO THE CENTRE. FILL IN THE MISSING LETTERS TO FIND OUT WHAT IT IS.

A	R	L
?	Y	?
N	E	G

Puzzle Four

Maths Riddle - 15 points for a correct answer

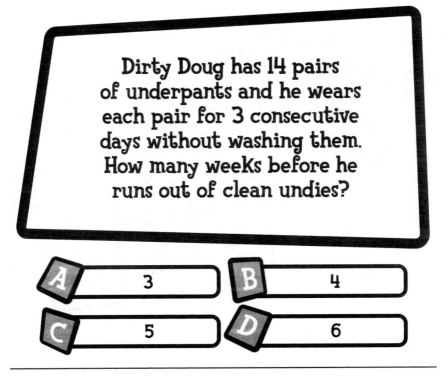

Dirty Doug has 14 pairs of underpants and he wears each pair for 3 consecutive days without washing them. How many weeks before he runs out of clean undies?

A 3

B 4

C 5

D 6

Puzzle Five

Number Puzzle - 25 points for a correct answer

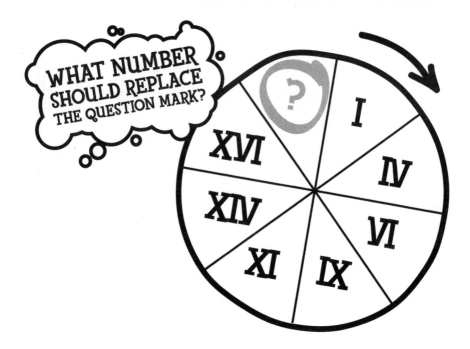

Puzzle Six

Sudoku Puzzle - 35 points for a correct answer

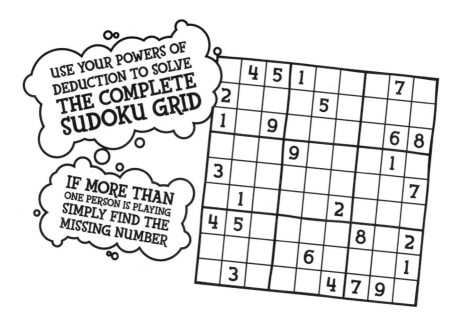

USE YOUR POWERS OF DEDUCTION TO SOLVE THE COMPLETE SUDOKU GRID

IF MORE THAN ONE PERSON IS PLAYING SIMPLY FIND THE MISSING NUMBER

Game Fourteen - Answers

Should your brain be crumbled or congratulated?

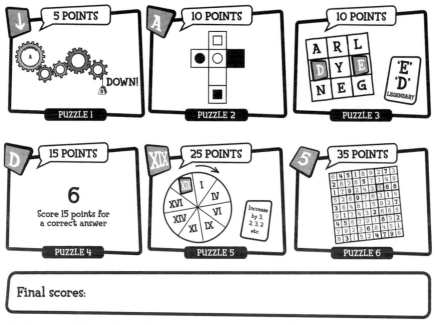

5 POINTS

DOWN!

PUZZLE 1

10 POINTS

PUZZLE 2

10 POINTS

A R L
D Y E
N E G

'E'
'D'
LEGENDARY

PUZZLE 3

15 POINTS

6

Score 15 points for
a correct answer

PUZZLE 4

25 POINTS

XIX I IV
XVI   VI
XIV XI IX

Increase
by 3,
2, 3, 2
etc.

PUZZLE 5

35 POINTS

PUZZLE 6

Final scores:

Go to page 167 and check out where you rate on the Brain Scale.

Game Fifteen

It's time you unlocked some of those gray cells
and let your brains out for some exercise.

Puzzle One

Brain Maze - 5 points for a correct answer

Puzzle Two

Weights/Values - 10 points for a correct answer

(i)

(ii)

x8

HOW MANY **APPLES** WILL BALANCE FIGURE (iii)?

(iii)

A: 2   B: 4   C: 8   D: 6

Puzzle Three

Word Puzzle - 10 points for a correct answer

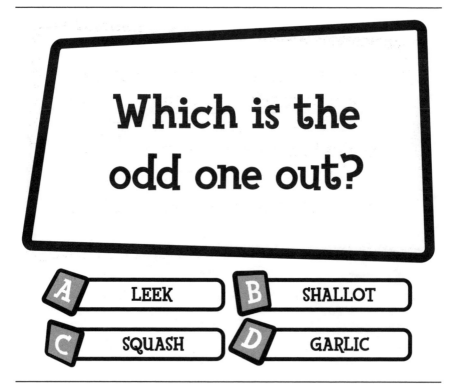

Which is the odd one out?

A LEEK

B SHALLOT

C SQUASH

D GARLIC

Puzzle Four

Maths Riddle - 15 points for a correct answer

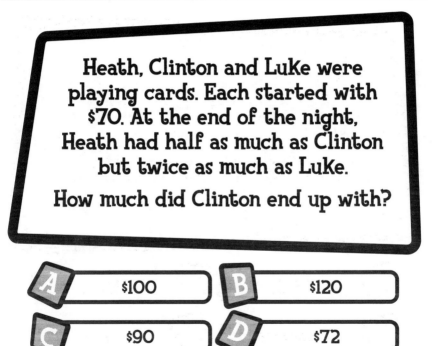

Heath, Clinton and Luke were playing cards. Each started with $70. At the end of the night, Heath had half as much as Clinton but twice as much as Luke.

How much did Clinton end up with?

A $100

B $120

C $90

D $72

Puzzle Five

Number Puzzle - 25 points for a correct answer

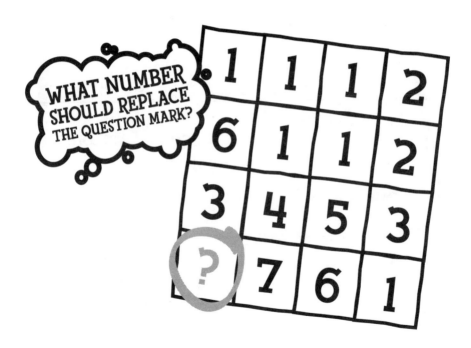

Puzzle Six

Sudoku Puzzle - 35 points for a correct answer

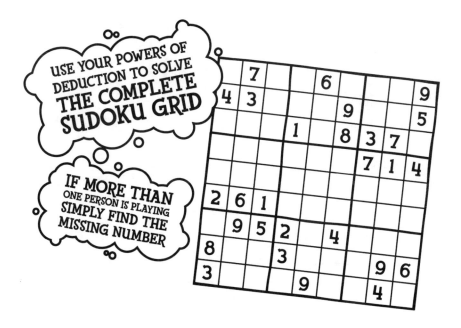

USE YOUR POWERS OF DEDUCTION TO SOLVE THE COMPLETE SUDOKU GRID

IF MORE THAN ONE PERSON IS PLAYING SIMPLY FIND THE MISSING NUMBER

Game Fifteen - Answers

Brains are 85% water, which is why you may have steam coming out your ears.

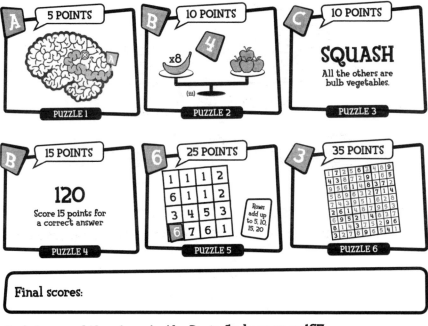

A | **5 POINTS**

PUZZLE 1

B | **10 POINTS**

x8   4

(iii)

PUZZLE 2

C | **10 POINTS**

SQUASH

All the others are
bulb vegetables.

PUZZLE 3

B | **15 POINTS**

120

Score 15 points for
a correct answer

PUZZLE 4

6 | **25 POINTS**

1	1	1	2
6	1	1	2
3	4	5	3
6	7	6	1

Rows
add up
to 5, 10,
15, 20

PUZZLE 5

3 | **35 POINTS**

1	7	2	5	6	3	4	8	9
4	3	8	7	2	9	1	6	5
9	5	6	1	4	8	3	7	2
5	8	9	6	3	2	7	1	4
7	4	3	9	5	1	6	2	8
2	6	1	4	8	7	9	5	3
6	9	5	2	1	4	8	3	7
8	1	4	3	7	5	2	9	6
3	2	7	8	9	6	5	4	1

PUZZLE 6

Final scores:

Cool down and then turn to the Brain Scale on page 167.

Game Sixteen

Apparently the more you use your brain, the better it works. Or have your scores so far proved the opposite?

Puzzle One

Cognitive Therapy - 5 points for a correct answer

Puzzle Two

Match Shape - 10 points for a correct answer

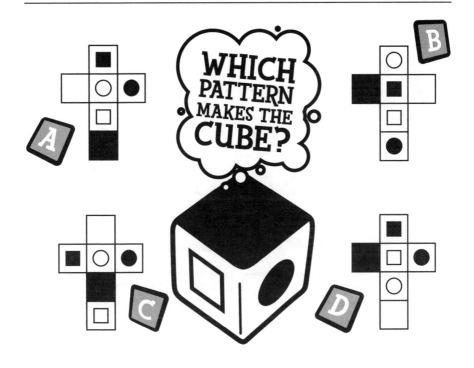

Puzzle Three

Word Puzzle - 10 points for a correct answer

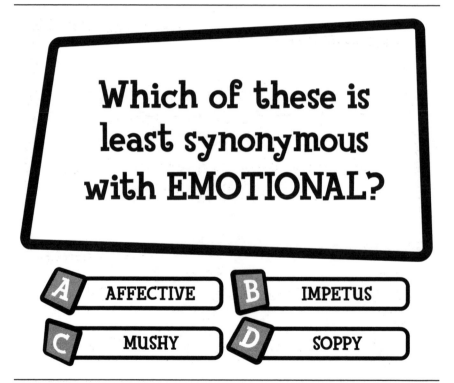

Which of these is least synonymous with EMOTIONAL?

A AFFECTIVE

B IMPETUS

C MUSHY

D SOPPY

Puzzle Four

Maths Riddle - 15 points for a correct answer

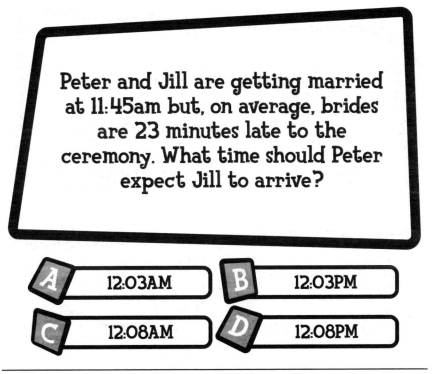

Peter and Jill are getting married at 11:45am but, on average, brides are 23 minutes late to the ceremony. What time should Peter expect Jill to arrive?

A 12:03AM

B 12:03PM

C 12:08AM

D 12:08PM

Puzzle Five

Number Puzzle - 25 points for a correct answer

Puzzle Six

Sudoku Puzzle - 35 points for a correct answer

USE YOUR POWERS OF DEDUCTION TO SOLVE THE COMPLETE SUDOKU GRID

IF MORE THAN ONE PERSON IS PLAYING SIMPLY FIND THE MISSING NUMBER

Game Sixteen - Answers

It's time to see who wins the title of 'The Brainiest Brain in the Room'.

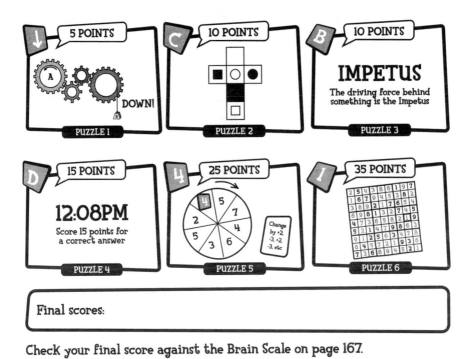

5 POINTS

DOWN!

PUZZLE 1

10 POINTS

PUZZLE 2

10 POINTS

IMPETUS

The driving force behind
something is the Impetus

PUZZLE 3

15 POINTS

12:08PM

Score 15 points for
a correct answer

PUZZLE 4

25 POINTS

Change
by +2,
-3, +2,
-3, etc

PUZZLE 5

35 POINTS

PUZZLE 6

Final scores:

Check your final score against the Brain Scale on page 167.

Game Seventeen

Now come on, lift your game.
IQ does not stand for "I Quit!"

Puzzle One

Brain Maze - 5 points for a correct answer

Puzzle Two

Weights/Values - 10 points for a correct answer

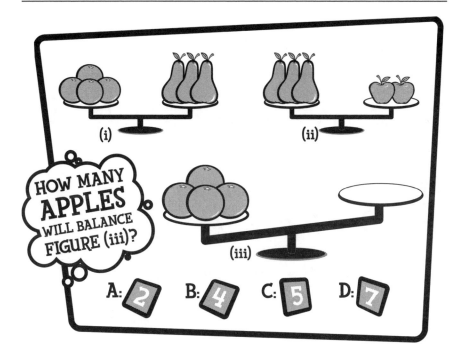

HOW MANY **APPLES** WILL BALANCE FIGURE (iii)?

A: 2   B: 4   C: 5   D: 7

Puzzle Three

Word Grid - 10 points for a correct answer

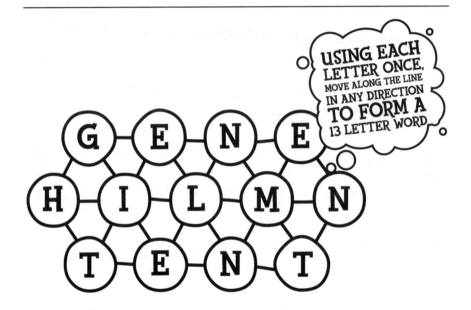

Puzzle Four

Maths Riddle - 15 points for a correct answer

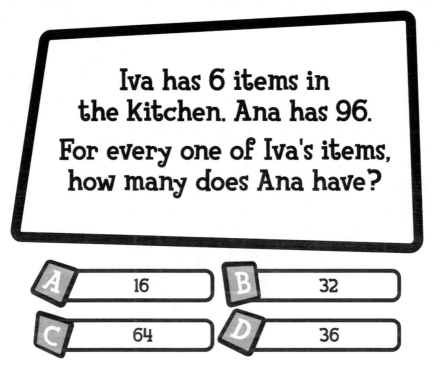

Iva has 6 items in
the Kitchen. Ana has 96.

For every one of Iva's items,
how many does Ana have?

A 16

B 32

C 64

D 36

Puzzle Five

Number Puzzle - 25 points for a correct answer

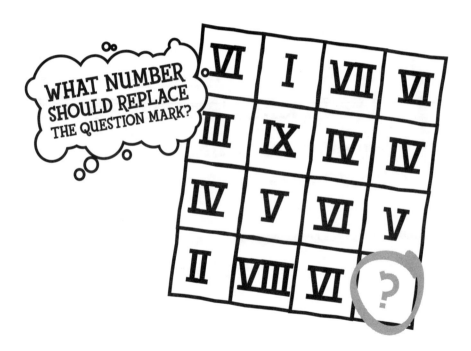

WHAT NUMBER SHOULD REPLACE THE QUESTION MARK?

Puzzle Six

Sudoku Puzzle - 35 points for a correct answer

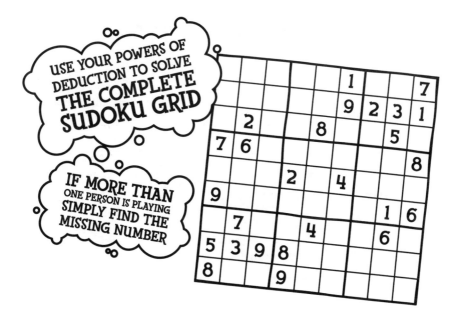

USE YOUR POWERS OF DEDUCTION TO SOLVE **THE COMPLETE SUDOKU GRID**

IF MORE THAN ONE PERSON IS PLAYING **SIMPLY FIND THE MISSING NUMBER**

Game Seventeen - Answers

OK ... are you an Einstein or a Frankenstein? ... an egghead or an air-head?

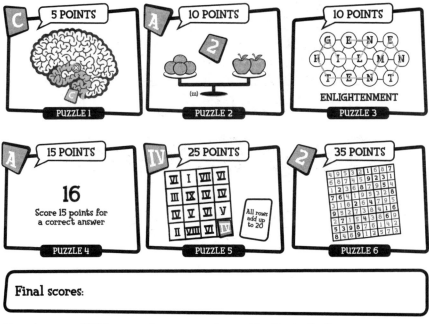

PUZZLE 1 — C — 5 POINTS

PUZZLE 2 — A — 10 POINTS
(iii)

PUZZLE 3 — 10 POINTS
ENLIGHTENMENT

PUZZLE 4 — A — 15 POINTS
16
Score 15 points for a correct answer

PUZZLE 5 — IV — 25 POINTS
All rows add up to 20

PUZZLE 6 — 2 — 35 POINTS

Final scores:

Turn to page 167 to see where you rate on the Brain Scale.

Game Eighteen

This one should really sort the neurons from the old.
How will you rate?

Puzzle One

Cognitive Therapy - 5 points for a correct answer

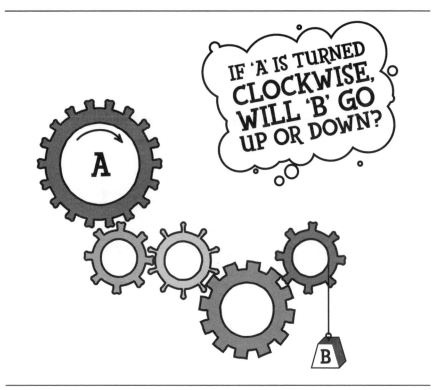

Puzzle Two

Match Shape - 10 points for a correct answer

Puzzle Three

Word Puzzle - 10 points for a correct answer

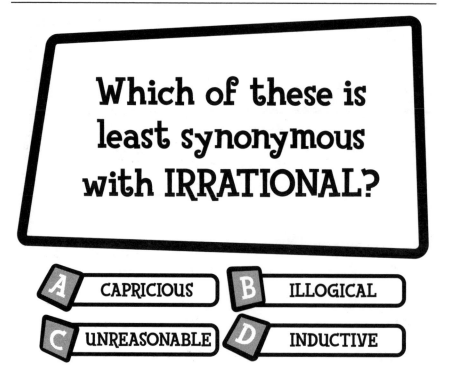

Which of these is least synonymous with IRRATIONAL?

A CAPRICIOUS

B ILLOGICAL

C UNREASONABLE

D INDUCTIVE

Puzzle Four

Maths Riddle - 15 points for a correct answer

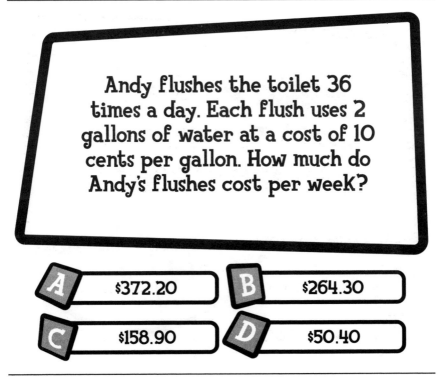

Andy flushes the toilet 36 times a day. Each flush uses 2 gallons of water at a cost of 10 cents per gallon. How much do Andy's flushes cost per week?

A $372.20

B $264.30

C $158.90

D $50.40

Puzzle Five

Number Puzzle - 25 points for a correct answer

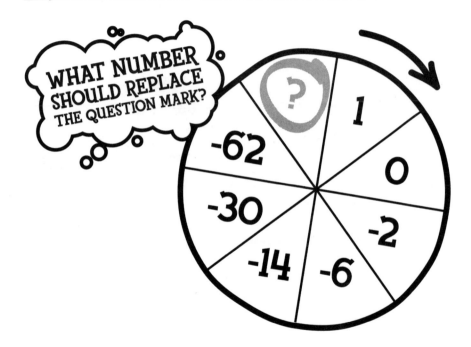

Puzzle Six

Sudoku Puzzle - 35 points for a correct answer

USE YOUR POWERS OF DEDUCTION TO SOLVE THE COMPLETE SUDOKU GRID

IF MORE THAN ONE PERSON IS PLAYING SIMPLY FIND THE MISSING NUMBER

Game Eighteen - Answers

Let's sort the dons from the dunces, the masterminds from the never-minds.

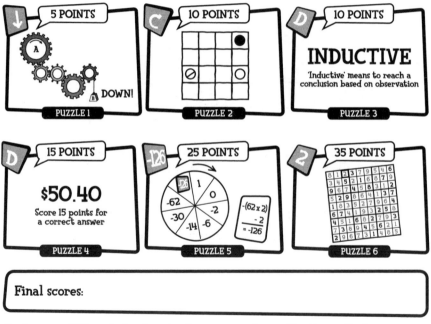

PUZZLE 1 — 5 POINTS
A DOWN!

PUZZLE 2 — 10 POINTS

PUZZLE 3 — 10 POINTS
INDUCTIVE
'Inductive' means to reach a conclusion based on observation

PUZZLE 4 — 15 POINTS
$50.40
Score 15 points for a correct answer

PUZZLE 5 — 25 POINTS
-126
1
0
-62
-2
-30
-14
-6
-(62 x 2)
- 2
= -126

PUZZLE 6 — 35 POINTS

Final scores:

Go to page 167 and check out where you rate on the Brain Scale.

Game Ninteen

Your workout in the gymnasium of the mind
is nearly at an end. Give it all you've got!

Puzzle One

Brain Maze - 5 points for a correct answer

Puzzle Two

Weights/Values - 10 points for a correct answer

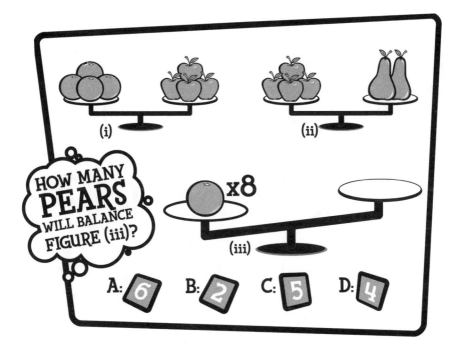

(i)

(ii)

HOW MANY **PEARS** WILL BALANCE FIGURE (iii)?

x8

(iii)

A: 6   B: 2   C: 5   D: 4

Puzzle Three

Word Puzzle - 10 points for a correct answer

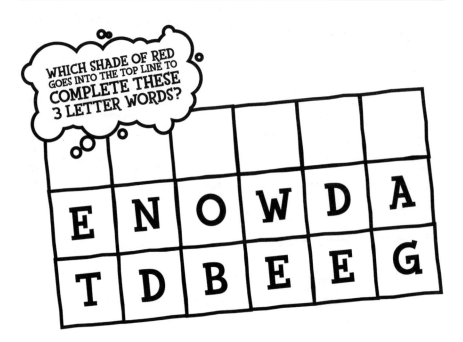

WHICH SHADE OF RED GOES INTO THE TOP LINE TO COMPLETE THESE 3 LETTER WORDS?

E	N	O	W	D	A
T	D	B	E	E	G

Puzzle Four

Maths Riddle - 15 points for a correct answer

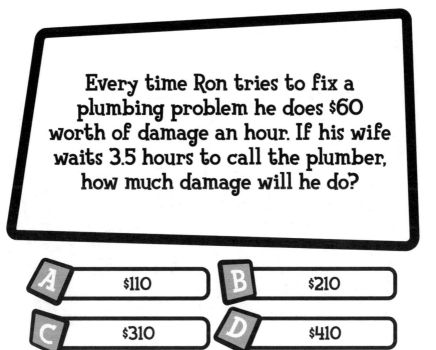

Every time Ron tries to fix a plumbing problem he does $60 worth of damage an hour. If his wife waits 3.5 hours to call the plumber, how much damage will he do?

A. $110

B. $210

C. $310

D. $410

Puzzle Five

Number Puzzle - 25 points for a correct answer

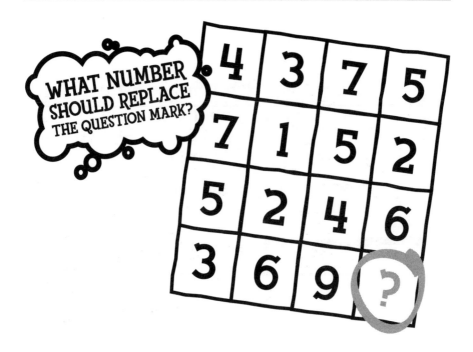

WHAT NUMBER SHOULD REPLACE THE QUESTION MARK?

4	3	7	5
7	1	5	2
5	2	4	6
3	6	9	?

Puzzle Six

Sudoku Puzzle - 35 points for a correct answer

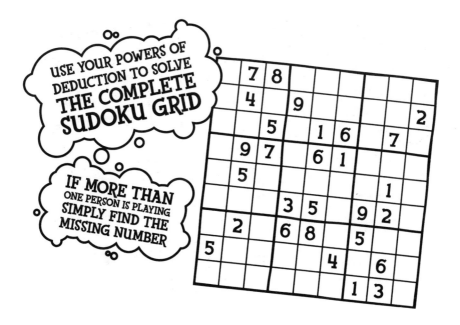

USE YOUR POWERS OF DEDUCTION TO SOLVE THE COMPLETE SUDOKU GRID

IF MORE THAN ONE PERSON IS PLAYING SIMPLY FIND THE MISSING NUMBER

Game Ninteen - Answers

Whose brain will reign supreme?
Remember! The more you play the smarter you'll become.

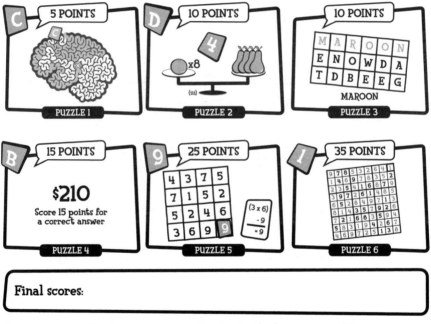

PUZZLE 1 — C — 5 POINTS

PUZZLE 2 — D — 10 POINTS — ×8 (iii)

PUZZLE 3 — 10 POINTS
MAROON
| E | N | O | W | D | A |
| T | D | B | E | E | G |
MAROON

PUZZLE 4 — B — 15 POINTS
$210
Score 15 points for a correct answer

PUZZLE 5 — 9 — 25 POINTS
4	3	7	5
7	1	5	2
5	2	4	6
3	6	9	9
(3 × 6)
- 9
= 9

PUZZLE 6 — I — 35 POINTS

Final scores:

Compare your final score against the Brain Scale on page 167.

158

Game Twenty

Just because you have an open mind doesn't mean you have nothing between the ears ... or does it? This is your last chance to find out. Make it count!

Puzzle One

Brain Maze - 5 points for a correct answer

Puzzle Two

Match Shape - 10 points for a correct answer

Puzzle Three

Word Grid - 10 points for a correct answer

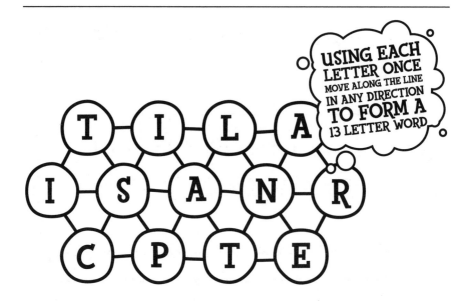

USING EACH LETTER ONCE MOVE ALONG THE LINE IN ANY DIRECTION TO FORM A 13 LETTER WORD

Puzzle Four

Maths Riddle - 15 points for a correct answer

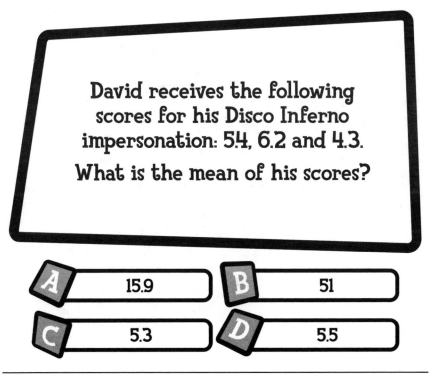

David receives the following scores for his Disco Inferno impersonation: 5.4, 6.2 and 4.3.

What is the mean of his scores?

A 15.9

B 51

C 5.3

D 5.5

Puzzle Five

Number Puzzle - 25 points for a correct answer

Puzzle Six

Sudoku Puzzle - 35 points for a correct answer

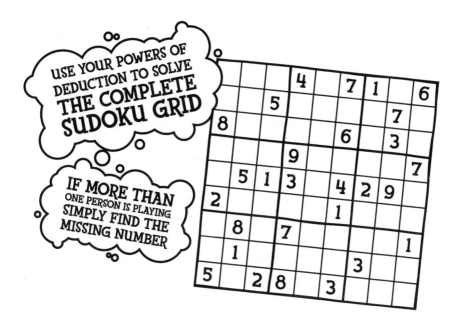

USE YOUR POWERS OF DEDUCTION TO SOLVE THE COMPLETE SUDOKU GRID

IF MORE THAN ONE PERSON IS PLAYING SIMPLY FIND THE MISSING NUMBER

Game Twenty - Answers

Is your brain as dead as a dodo, or a wonderful gift to the universe?

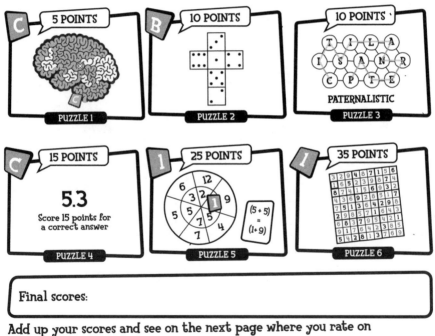

5 POINTS — PUZZLE 1

10 POINTS — PUZZLE 2

10 POINTS — PATERNALISTIC — PUZZLE 3

15 POINTS

5.3

Score 15 points for a correct answer

PUZZLE 4

25 POINTS

(5 + 5) = (1 + 9)

PUZZLE 5

35 POINTS — PUZZLE 6

Final scores:

Add up your scores and see on the next page where you rate on the evolutionary scale.

The Brain Scale

Take a deep breath, check your final score against the scale below and see if your gray matter really matters or not.

0 = Pet Rock
Too bad ... you have the analytical skills of a pet rock. On the upside, you're simply brilliant at just sitting there and doing your thing, which appears to be nothing! I guess when you've hit 'rock' bottom, the only way is up.

10 = Dodo
Unfortunately you have the brains of a dodo! Don't worry, you're not extinct yet, but you're not taking off in a hurry either! Keep playing The Brain Game my fine feathered friend, you can only get smarter.

20 - 30 = Busy Bee
Well done ... your brain is like a busy little bee. Part of a team, you flit from flower to flower, buzzing away with a happy smile on your face. If you paid attention to what you're meant to be doing, you'd be the queen of the hive.

40 - 50 = Primate
Nice one, monkey brains. You know how to use the tools, but unfortunately you think you're smarter than you really are - in fact, you're driving everyone absolutely bananas!

60 - 70 = Elephant
An elephant never forgets. And it appears that brains of a pachyderm have been packed into your head. You're either very clever, or you've played this game before and memorized the puzzles! Something to trumpet about, eh?

80 - 90 = Humpback Whale
With the gray matter of a humpback whale, over three times bigger than the average human, I'm surprised you don't have a big head. But then again, maybe you do? Now that's some big brain!

100 = You are the Brain!
It's completely unheard of. You are not from this world. You should bottle your brain and sell it. It would be selfish not to share such a wondrous intellect with the entire universe. You are THE BRAIN.

Notes

Notes

Notes

Notes

Notes

Notes

Hall of Fame

The names and scores entered here are living proof that some people have bigger brains than others, some make better use of what they have, and some are quite prepared to cheat.

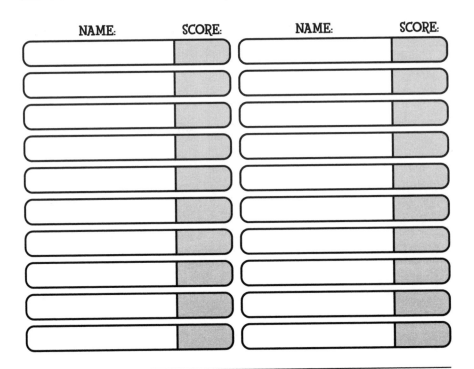

NAME:	SCORE:	NAME:	SCORE:

Hall of Shame

If your name and score is entered here, the real shame would be if you didn't use this humiliating experience to try and do better next time. Of course, it may be that you really are dumb.

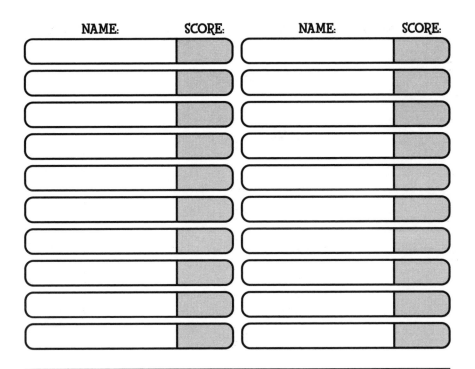

NAME:	SCORE:	NAME:	SCORE: